The Chosen Garden

by

MICHEAL O'SIADHAIL

The Dedalus Press
24 The Heath, Cypress Downs, Dublin 6W

ISBN 0 948268 87 5 (Paper)
ISBN 0 948268 88 3 (Bound)

Other poetry collections by Micheal O'Siadhail include:
"Springnight" 1983
"The Image Wheel" 1985

Cover Painting: "Garden Green" by Norah McGuinness, courtesy, the Hugh Lane Municipal Gallery of Modern Art, Dublin, and Rhoda McGuinness.

ACKNOWLEDGEMENTS:
Acknowledgements are due to the editors of the following where some of these poems appeared for the first time:
Chapman, The Honest Ulsterman, Irish Times, Irish University Review, Keltoi, Krino, Limerick Broadsheet, New Welsh Review, Orbis, Poetry Australia, Poetry Ireland Review, Southern Humanities Review, Sunday Tribune, Stand.
"Those Whom We Follow" was originally commissioned and broadcast by RTE as part of a song cycle The Naked Flame (with Seoirse Bodley).

The Dedalus Press receives financial assistance from An Chomhairle Ealaíon, The Arts Council, Ireland.

CONTENTS

I Departure

Espousal   11
Initiation   13
Visit   14
Foster-Figure   15
Shoulder-High   16
Fallen Angel   17
Old Wine   18
A Harsher Light   19

II A Blurred Music

Youth   23
Hesitation   25
Questing   26
Manhood   27
Spilling   29
Reflection   30

III Fists of Stone

Wanderers   33
Stranger   34
Folksong   36
Coastlines   37
Leavetaking   38
Timepiece   40
In Memoriam Máirtín Ó Cadhain   42
Visionary   44
Dark   45

IV Turns and Returns

History   49
Belonging   50
Underworld   51
Probing   53
Vision   55
High Tide   56
Freedom   57
Those We Follow   58
Touchstone   59
Return   60

V Rerooting

Journeys   65
Beginnings   66
A Presence   67
An Unfolding   68
Squall   69
The Other Voice   70
Out of the Blue   71
St. Brigid's Cross   72
While You are Talking   73
Hindsight   74
A Circle   75

VI Opening Out

Disclosure   79
Grantchester Meadows   80
Motet   82
Train Journey   83
Kinsmen   84
Matins   85
Perspectives   86
Memory   88
Hail! Madam Jazz   90
Child   91

for Vigdis and Erik, Deborah and David,
under whose roofs I've rested;
for Brid
whose roof I share

I

DEPARTURE

Baciami sulla bocca, ultima estate.
Dimmi che non andrai tanto lontano.
Retorna con l'amore sulle spalle,
ed il tuo peso non sará piú vano.

Kiss me on the mouth, final summer.
Tell me you will not go far away.
Come back with love on your shoulders,
and your weight will no longer be in vain.

Sandro Penna
(trans. Alessandro Gentili
and Catherine O'Brien)

Espousal
Initiation
Visit
Foster-Figure
Shoulder-High
Fallen Angel
Old Wine
A Harsher Light

ESPOUSAL

Days early my trousseau lay in the hallway,
Mother's own school trunk newly hinged,
freighted as prescribed — all regalia
taped and numbered: rug, napkin ring,
tuck box, laundry bags. Hour by hour
a dreamy September holds its breath.

Late evening, a scuffle of gravel as cars
brake on the castle's forecourt. Novices
reconnoitre, bustle of arrivals, goodbyes,
last advices and already I fidget, eager
to embrace my venture; parting promises:
a visit in a fortnight; waves in the half-light.

Down the marble steps into the vast
corridor of wainscotting and notice boards,
lists of placings for study-hall and chapel;
chance meetings, the territory explored —
playrooms, libraries. The tug of a bell,
a hush and we file towards night prayers.

So, this is the honeymoon of my fantasy,
a reverie of quads, pillow fights, decent
chaps with parcels and cads in Coventry....
My friend was coming, I begged to be sent.
'You're on your own', father has warned,
'you've made your bed, now lie in it'.

Ten twenty. Lights out in the Holy Angels,
we slide into iron beds; a skittish
silence falls; in earshot another dormitory,
same prayer, commanding flick of switch.
Neighbours whisper introductions: Michael
Walls, Roscommon; Flannery from Tipperary.

Snatches of a parlance, subliminal spells:
all out, lectio brevis, night-squares,
smoke in the mind; days to come
gleam, a jingling clump of mortise keys.
I espouse a new world, drop into sleep;
expectation whirrs in the tongues of bells.

INITIATION

By hearsay beginners fear the passage rite:
dark talk of toilet dousing and shamings.
Watch your step. Last year's weaklings lord
a brief revenge — *old scout's preference.*
To endure is everything, so now bide time.
Day by day the hierarchical bluff is called.
Seats at table fixed by scramble, the head
holds sway, portions out the food at whim,
waylaying second helpings for his table-top
cronies. It's Monday. Roly-poly and custard
for dessert; O'Sullivan acts the tough, threatens
to confiscate my share.... Outside I tackle him;
a flurry of punches, I fall in a stranglehold.
Days later another flare-up; again he wins.
His taboo endangered, we have settled down
to a sultry peace. Fantasy slips into reality.
Inmates of a world slowly, slowly enamoured
of our narrow purlieus, every rule and loophole,
bounds and out of bounds, little by little
we grow fond of our containment. After dinner
in the hamper-room cutting a slice of cake
one of *the hards* comes wheedling, menacing
give us a scrounge! Swear at him loudly —
grinning, he moves on. The weeks pass,
the fittest thrive. No Joyce, no Stephen Dedalus,
your ghost may sulk on the Third Line crease,
baulk at our scramble, but your gaze is hindsight.
We think we dream of home and all the while
who got *sleeps* or a parcel, who made the team,
shifts of comradeship, rumours of a prefect's mood,
concerns, subterfuges map our hours and fill
an atlas of our living. We're in love with survival.
All other worlds are slipping out of reach.

VISIT

Sunday afternoon about three o'clock
('with prior permission from your prefect')
pewed in a car on the gravel forecourt
our talk swivels between two worlds.
Angling herself in the passenger seat
my mother turns her face to me;
awkward behind a steering wheel, father's
eye catches mine in his rear-view mirror.

I rehearse this scene trying to read
my mother's face wondering if she sensed
I had left for good — son and emigré.
Four months' days ticked off a calendar,
at last I'd return, a displaced guest,
uneasy with neighbours, missing school friends,
my eye proportioned to halls and arches
and home diminished as a doll's house.

Family doings, bulletins from a neighbourhood,
mention of names, small emissaries
of emotion from suburban roads, old
gravities draw me for a moment homeward.
And I resist. We are visitors for each other.
Unwittingly those weeks of initiation leave
a baffle between us. Our words fall short.
I am learning a new language, another lore.

FOSTER-FIGURE

Even now there is some enigma
in that glance. Though long grown
beyond a first self-surrender
or cooler reappraisals, I prize
his affirmation, always revere him.

Odd how I had found favour.
Did he know I craved the nurture
of his words? I fall on my feet:
prodigy, prize-winner, captain,
a protegé moving in his slipstream.

Surely among my fosterers
he laid the lightest of hands;
strings until then silent
in a father's shortfall of sanction
stirring trembled toward song.

I probe the essence of this energy;
no blandishments or blind approval,
his unblinking trust enticed me,
fingered some awareness of worth;
in his praise all is possible.

Though at first a copycat tremor,
after many storms I'll still
strum the chord of his assurance,
that music I'll make my own,
an old resonance I'll summon up.

SHOULDER-HIGH

An image shapes those winter afternoons:
our breath plumes the frost as we drill
scrumming down over the stud-pocked mud.

A sweaty rapture heaves and shoves,
furies of willpower rise moonlike
in the mind and we bullock inches forward.

Faith in flawless moves, elusive flashes,
clay feet as light as angels' wings you race
and race and dream immortal touch-downs.

'Run it !', the crowd urged, 'run with it!' —
around men's jostling shoulders you'd glimpsed
a winger arcing inwards to the corner flag;

whistles, rattles, horns, coloured scarfs
flung in loops of glory, we'd stamped
as a train rumbled under the stand.

A thumping bell: *wumba, wumba, wumba,*
ging, gang, shoulder-high down the marble steps
ride the conquerors. Three cheers for the captain!

Dusk. Like tapdancers we clack the bootroom's
terrazzo, sit musing fleshy and happy
plucking soil from between the studs of our boots.

FALLEN ANGEL

Returning another autumn we discover
a changed regime, a community reshuffled;
losing my sponsors in that shake-up,
roots too shallow, I fall from grace.

New brooms with fresh sweeps.
How easily we become how we're seen;
failure throws an oblong shadow,
I cover hurts with a jaunty humour,

pretend not to care, affect disdain,
harden the core to day-by-day
humiliations — tiny erosions of respect —
learn the slow rustings of shame.

And laugh a bitter laugh! while inside
discs of trust skew and warp.
Where can you turn? You've made your bed,
now lie there widower to your dream.

How many faces must a wound wear?
Iconoclast, windmill-tilter, self-saboteur,
stunted years of a poise too hard won;
yet in such moves the spiral turns....

Nothing. A squall in a child's cup!
But you're the child, this is your cup.
I own no master. My gods of innocence
fallen, I clench a fragile self-reliance.

OLD WINE

Another October, middle-aged, black-dressed,
urbane. It will have been mid-June we last
shared refectory tables, years of crumbs
wedged in their grooves. Dream beyond terms,
hopes, fears, expectations. A quarter century:
rub-a-dub and who do you think we'll be?

A stranger, a handshake, a name spoken.
Imagine swathes of hair, gawky enthusiasm.
Maybe it's the voice's fall I recognize?
How the mind plays tricks: mouth, eyes
begin to resemble memory turned hindsight;
this was the story to be, the face to fit

a brewer, a banker, a hotelkeeper. We swap
life-tales. (Will some shy away — black sheep,
the loners?) Five years apart for each year
I'd spent there. Some shaft sunk together
into our early earth, a corridor of fondness
moistens, wells. An old yearning openness.

'Are you happy?', I dare. 'Well maybe not
the way I'd dreamt, I just accept my lot.'
A face that suffered. Another recalls rivalry
others remember differently. Let it by:
nexus of myths, fictions to which we cling,
wine of fables spilt deftly on the tongue.

Blue cheese, swirls of cigar smoke and guffaws;
a toast, our madcap heckling, boisterous applause.
The past is present. Confirm me class-brother;
ghosts we tame and need or crave to lay together.
Addresses, promises and I'm full of at-one-ness,
of alone-ness. Warmth flickers in a glass.

A HARSHER LIGHT

There we were, blazers and whites,
hands thrust in our pockets as we talked,
figures from a faded epoch that final
long summer term before the scattering.
Suddenly in the cram and grind of exams,
a hurried leavetaking and all was over.

Soon new realities are shaping.
Dumbfounded how readily we trusted,
took childhood's caste for granted.
We sort our memories, deftly rework
once certainties to mould conscious
visions of perfection, in hindsight

deplore that old man emptying slops,
our servant *Johnnies*, menial Brothers
(even in the graveyard serried *Paters*
and *Fraters* never mingled). At late-
night parties raising mugs of wine
we'll sing *There but for fortune....*

Bohemia, that counterworld is waiting,
unlatching its oyster of adventure; yet
entering the lonely labyrinth of choice,
for all the bravado, in spite of disavowal,
on the sly I rue the loss of an ordinance
open-and-shut, an inmate's bitter-sweet.

II

A BLURRED MUSIC

Come sarebbe belle il mondo
        se ci fosse una regola
    par girare nei labirinti.

How beautiful the world would be
        if there were a procedure
    for moving through labyrinths.

                    Umberto Eco

Youth
Hesitation
Questing
Manhood
Spilling
Reflection

YOUTH

Break boyhood's taboo,
step on every line
to crack a devil's cup.
Hurts turn to arrogance.
We're naked and brazen
under the skies.

Our gods can wait.
No need for hurry.
Old wisdoms painfully unfold;
sooner or later
will we return, fumbling
from clue to clue?

Amazing how the gods
will choose to gamble,
hanging our destinies
on such flimsy plots
as we stumble on a trail,
children on a paper chase.

Gestures, even intonations,
quirks of our childhood
heroes, once imitated
now become our own,
we stitch together
a patchwork of self.

Maybe some hints,
prompts from deities:
a word of praise,
spin-offs from mistakes,
strangers we met,
women who chose us.

Hearing the jazz of chance
we advance, making
headway by detour.
In such journeys subsist
the working of our karma,
the whirling of our stars.

HESITATION

The first awestruck flutter. To think
another cares! Promised phone calls,
letters in tinted envelopes, presents
swapped, delicacies of dress, faint
traces of *Eau de Cologne*, a gentling
closeness; we nestled in such intimacies.

Meals *en famille*. A wealthy father
listens shyly to namedropping, tiny
attempts at creditworthiness, while
mother bestows protective luxury;
allows a sort of ease by implication;
we are children playing house.

But something is sowing a doubtseed:
an instinct maybe or scapegrace need
to abandon shelter, stretch a wing,
perhaps a dream of an Eve *fatale*
who waits to bite a forbidden apple.
Must we lose the comfort of the garden?

Then those long Spring evening walks;
wistful handholding, blushed words,
minor kisses in the porch, our dallied
goodnights. A last orchard tenderness
before passionate winds outside those walls
lift such timid blossoms towards pleasure.

QUESTING

A time for gaiety, a time to sunder
taken-for-granted gods, to flounder
or squander; a feckless valley-time
before we find a cause and climb
into the laps of countergods, a bizarre
time when in some Dublin bar,
arguing the toss as best we could,
we served our apprentice adulthood.

Till closing time we talked and talked;
the intellect now cock of the walk.
What does it mean? We interrogate
our upbringing, unravelling with apostate
zeal a web of code and token
and court our guilty ecstasy of broken
symbols, a dance along the precipice,
new and giddy pull of the abyss.

We leave, carrying our parcels of beer
across a sidestreet; someone for the sheer
hell heaves a brick at a windowpane —
we scuttle out of trouble down a lane
back to our meagre Bohemia to expound
meanings of the universe. Above the sound
of our voices a bedsitter radio is playing;
between stations, a blurred music sways.

MANHOOD

Soap the butts of the fingers, back straight,
knees bent, the shovel does the stooping;
whatever you do, keep scratching. The sagging
cement bag heaved from a shoulder thumps
deadweight on the dust, its layered paper
slit across the belly-bulge by angled
jabs of our shovels, each half then
tugged apart. *So you'll never
go back now, mate!* A bucket
swung by its handle, slops of water
puddle through grey powder, shovels
knead in the gravel, scooping, slicing.

Student? — the Clare ganger menaced
Jaysus no! Money, of course
(notes fanned and counted on a bed)
but more an expiation. Remember a first
shock hearing returned Araners
round on their children, shout in Cockney:
Shut your bloody mouths, wi' you!
Here they were in Pimlico. Blistered
palms atone for privilege, self-obliteration
mixing the powder with gravel. Back
straight, let the shovel do the bending;
scooping, slicing, working into one.

Out on top, you and the sledge —
orders from the ganger. Stories up
jauntily astride a sheer wall
Blacks are billowing brick and dust.
One breaks this rhythm to watch
my unsteady hands measure timid
swings for the sledge. *Hey,* he hoots,
hey! You paleface is yella!
Below, the ganger's arms beckon.
He rehearses a now ritual dismissal
(a nephew due next week from Clare),
You'll be finishing up tomorrow.

Friday at noon abandon duties,
search out another site, another
start. *Excuse me could you*
please tell me where... a bowler-hatted
man cuts a silent half-circle,
passes in disdain. Stung an instant —
a desire to pull rank, to rail,
tell him who you really are.... And
who may I ask are you, sir?
Smeared with gravel and limestone
(insignia of reparation), human and alone,
scan that London skyline for a crane.

SPILLING

Should we regret
our rush towards light?
Belligerent shoots of elder,

pimpled and taut, sun-
hungry jabbed upwards
through an old canopy.

Should we regret
a youth spent spilling
our bonebred innocence?

First water runs
through dry clay
yet trails of its moisture

clot the porous soil.
Earth thickens to trap
its second innocence.

REFLECTION

Surely we fell for the self in the other,
our sweet will a mirror admiration;
fellows in intensity, our volatile attraction,
quick countersigns of likeness.

Fringe and lashes gleamed in laughter;
with swoops of black hair shoulder-length
she jutted her head rebelliously; behind
her jerky gladness a frailty lurks.

She stood on a table, sang *O rise
up lovely Sweeney*, every note
a theft, a spilt life — her nerves
spinning out that spalpeen's odyssey.

Under her command the room quivers.
(Did we fear for the spendthrift spirit?)
All in my youth and prime we drift
together *from the clear daylight till dawn.*

How blindingly we travelled. Confess
hindsight: maybe less love more desire,
a sullenness uncoiling moist and grateful.
'All my men were lonely', she said,

'all my men were driven' — her generous
mandate to caress the loner, to tempt,
to take, to rock, to slack, to lull
a moment in forgetfulness. How blindingly

at one, at odds, our humours shuttled —
loving or rowing — forever caught
in ironies of likeness; a self-recognition
drawing us together, pulling us apart.

III

FISTS OF STONE

Was there ever a cause too lost,
Ever a cause that was lost too long,
Or showed with the lapse of time too vain
For the generous tears of youth and song?

Robert Frost

Wanderers
Stranger
Folksong
Coastlines
Leavetaking
Timepiece
In Memoriam Máirtín Ó Cadhain
Visionary
Dark

WANDERERS

O saga of all that has happened
we know the tales and still
must we too be wanderers?

Gilgamesh strikes out for glory,
journeying to the Land of Cedars
to fight the giant Humbaba.

Redresser of wrongs, grasper
at golden shadows, Quixote
the knight is spurring his horse.

Is it then the same story:
a bid to shortcut history,
our scattergood craving for Eden?

Heroic or errant, do we loop
the loop or does goddess life
love the intensity of our tour?

Watch over us on our travels
o saga of all that has happened
if we must be such wanderers.

STRANGER

A youngster I came, pilgrim to the source;
fables of a native bliss stirred mottoes:
a land without a tongue, a land without a soul.
As the currachs drew alongside the steamer
men in dark blue shirts shouted exotic words.

In the kitchen a daughter returned on holiday
switches from her mother's tongue to chide
her London children. As I listen it seems
I am foreign to both, neither fish nor flesh.
Was I to be a stranger in this promised land?

I slip into a glove of language. But there's still
a vividness, an older mood, small courtesies
to fortune: the sea must have its own — to swim
is to challenge fate. Child of reason and will
I am at most a sojourner in that mind.

Talk then of the mainland as *the world outside,*
enter and become a citizen of this stony room:
handkerchief fields claimed from rocks, dung
dried for fuel, unmortared boulder walls,
calfskin shoes, stark artifices of survival.

A widower welcomes my visits, opens his sorrow
to the incomer. Gauchely, I mention his loneliness:
Hadn't he his turn? ask two neighbour women
swirling their petticoats *What ails him?*
they banter, standing in the sunshaft of a doorway.

One evening on the flags dancing starts up;
no music, island women summering from Boston
lilt reels, long to be courted. But men
shy of plaid skirts or lipstick don't dare
(still too boyish, subtleties pass me by).

Nudges and smothered laughter among the men.
Over again the word *stranger*. I bridle,
yearn to be an insider, unconsciously begin
a changeling life; turning a live-in lover
I wear my second nature, a grafted skin.

FOLKSONG

The voice is the only music that says what it tells
When I go to the Lonely Well I sit and anguish....
A message stretching its tendrils to memory calls,

summons up echoes, as if the bereft — the vanished
or absorbed — are naming their ghosts, a medley
of losers: Picts, Mayas, tribes of the Suquamish....

The singer quavers out that one love's agony,
cranks its rhythms out of a neighbour's hand:
the undertwang of the music keeps shifting the story.

The sap running in the pine carries the red man's
sacred meaning, the water's murmur is the voice
of his father's father; the white man takes this land

but all things share the one breath. The poise
of the dispossessed freights and lifts the turns,
tuning each line to the same plaintive noise.

Will the stones remember their feet, the seabirds
claw ogham epitaphs in the wriggled sand?
The singer winds down to the final spoken words.

A loneness in the shaft of the song refuses to end.

COASTLINES

A temperament takes on the world. I chose bleak
slabs of limestone, lone outcrops, promontories
poking their stubborn arms against an Atlantic;
supple elbows of strand seemed like cowardice.
Lines will blur, a seaboard fret and shift,
waves spending and being spent into the silence
of endless sands, rhythms of challenge and drift
husbanding or yielding the jigsaw shore of an island.
It's best the blue-grey rocks know nothing of how
constant water wears, a coiling uncoiling motion
flushing each snag or edge, ebb and flow
scouring the grain, their work being worked by ocean;
clenched fists of will jutted in their prime,
tangs of stone daring a tide or time.

LEAVETAKING

A moment balancing on a thwart,
then aboard the mainland steamer;
an islandman shook my hand,
laughed 'when you land, hide
all that Gaelic under a stone!'.

His words echoed. All over
the earth people are drifting
on this tide towards amber lights:
cities stretch out arms in greeting.
These were the giants we'd fight.

Was this Sancho Panza gainsaying?
Take care, your worship, they're
no giants but windmills, their arms
are sails whirled in the wind
to make the millstones turn.

But his worship could not hear;
zeal has its own defences: I knew
while in Boston fellow-countymen,
still too close to feel safe,
had scoffed at his broken English.

I clung mulishly to that world;
with the strange infatuation of rebuff —
that half-caste love — I claimed
my membership. (Leaving the school bus
someone jibes 'There goes the patriot'.)

Older I'd plead the cause:
an inheritance was sliding away.
If only I had been a treasurer
of fragments but all my youngness
willed that life to survive....

It was enough to love. We thought
the giants would fold their arms
and yield, as though nothing
could beat our stripling will:
youth and death were strangers.

Decades after in a city hospital
I interpret for an islandman. (At first
they'd thought him deaf: nurses
enunciate loudly, sign and gesture.)
The touring matron halting a moment

on rounds, speaks her *cupla focal*
and reverts. A face lightens and darkens
inwards. And how many days more?
Would he have to return? I hear
humiliation fall like a millstone.

The steamer cranks its anchor in
swamping the last creaks of wooden
thole-pins. Black-tarred coracles
ride accusingly out of reach:
I wear the skin not the flesh.

TIMEPIECE

Some gentleness seemed to mark her out among
the islanders. Days on end her talk mothered me.
Could I bring anything to thank her? I'd asked,
surely there was something she'd fancy? Childlike
in anticipation, pincering a thumb and forefinger
around her cuff, she'd mentioned a wristwatch.

I loved her toying delight as she watched
a golden arrow flicking its delicate seconds by.
A gift or a spoiling? Shudders of suburban grey,
the panic of clock-watching an unkillable time
counting down remorseless minutes, a millennium
of hours before a homecoming, turn of a latchkey.

There was, of course, the alarm with a yellowing face
and clumsy tick but mostly just her half-glance
at the angle of light in the door. Days tumble
into easy rituals, clearing of ashes, the thump
of sods in a bucket; even moments of gazing,
tiny flickers of meaning, fragments gathering.

I'd heard her tell the story of the sleeper's soul:
butterfly leaving his mouth to wander and return;
when he woke his dream had been the insect's journey.
Long afterwards a brain surgeon remarks how we explain
so narrowly, how maybe consciousness hovers beyond
the skull.... Does history toss our loss and gain?

It will all happen so quickly, one decade
catching a few centuries of Europe's change.
Off-the-peg chequered jackets begin to break
the uniform bawneen; a new buzz of motorcycles,
electric light, a screen perched in the corner,
exiles with newcomer wives return to settle.

'To set the hands, pull and twist it here' —
I took for granted. Fingers never focussed
on such smallness fumble about the winder.
Laughing aside the awkwardness, I take her wrist
where a tanned hand meets the white of arm
like a tide-mark, I tighten and buckle the strap.

IN MEMORIAM MÁIRTÍN Ó CADHAIN

Which face of many faces entranced
our fledgling time? Outsider
untamed and untamable, scorner of prudence,
blind and wide-eyed,
a hurt innocence striking out on every side.

Or was it a mirror-nature mothering
out stories to transcend
failure, lover of the blundering and the suffering
on this road without end,
a watching watchful eye stark and tender.

Those closing years, probing and embattled,
he sought somehow to wed
the avant garde with the vanishing, straddled
a destiny — a watershed,
new and old flirting and parting in that head.

Over Kirghiz, he broods as the engines swirled:
were high-haunched jets horses
riding to the Well at the End of the World? —
for no one knows
through what wild centuries roams back the rose?

The sweetsmelling heartbreaking rose.
He puzzles Oisín's tour to a zone
of youth, his touchdown to dust: 'who knows
maybe they'd foreshown
Einstein's time moving in a chamber of its own'.

Or the gritty humour? When the hearse stalled
we hoisted you shoulder high
slowing a mid-day city to a crawl;
laughing nearby,
a spirit rode the white steed skyward.

I see you returning ten generations on,
defiant and full of youth,
demanding how three hundred years have gone.
Tighten the saddle-girth;
your foot must never touch our island's earth.

VISIONARY

What was it then, what commanded such ardour?
A scattering of lonely islands, a few gnarled
seaboard townlands, underworld of a language frail
as patches of snow hiding in the shadows of a garden.

But the dwindling were so living. In this wonderland
of might-have-been I fell for the rhythm, the undertone
of my father's speech, built a golden dream.
(As you dreamt that land was falling asunder.)

A world as it is or a world as we want it:
when to resist old fate's take-for-granted
or when to submit; had I known before I slid
into a snowy fantasy, a fairyland of squander....

Was it a lavishness, a hankering for self-sacrifice,
part arrogance, part the need of the twice
shy for a paradise of the ideal, pure and beyond,
where one man's will turns a hag to a princess.

Oh, I was the fairy story's third son, the one
who, unlike his elder brothers would not shun
a hag by the roadside: surely I'd rub the ring,
summon a sword of light to slay the dragon.

Tell me now that land was a last outpost,
a straggling from another time no one's utmost
could save; the hungry beast of change roved
nearer, that vision was a ghost dance with the past.

Tell me now third brothers too have grown
older, have even learned to smile at highflown
dreams. Then tell me still somewhere in the thaw
a child is crying over a last island of snow.

DARK

When the god of childhood first fell
I tossed my hair over my shoulder;
there was a will, there was a way —
the sap rises, the tide fills
flushed with dreams of its own motion.

Now there's a will but no way,
must the sky with all its stars
rest stoically on these shoulders?
Did Atlas, loser of a golden
apple, resign and turn to stone?

No, not stone. Most of all
I fear the half-measure of greyness.
I choose the dark (or does the dark
choose me?) I want to fall,
open a chasm black and deep.

I plunge into an anarchy of gloom.
Can it be that dark before it slumps
conceives a light, prepares in its ruin
the already and not yet, heaves
long rhythms of chaos and creation?

But dark is dark: saddle of nothing
riding black hogs to the abyss.
Travel velvet spaces of despair;
terror, like a dredge, is scooping
out a void for love's surrender.

IV

TURNS AND RETURNS

Dark dreams in the dead of night
And on the reckless brow
Bent to let chaos in,
Tell that they shall come down,
Be broken, and rise again.

Edwin Muir

History
Belonging
Underworld
Probing
Vision
High Tide
Freedom
Those We Follow
Touchstone
Return

HISTORY

And we keep beginning afresh
an endless history
as if this odyssey
had never happened before. Yes,

ours was a spoiled generation
secure, even tepid
somehow untested —
no plague or war, torture or starvation.

Look how some were keeping faith
in a gulag while we
fumbled out our destiny,
walking our easy under-urban path.

So it wasn't their route (wince
at the thought). Still,
freedom was a crucible,
blundering chalkless tour in labyrinths.

Maybe we grope the same journey
scooping the oracular
in scandals of the particular
light we throw on some greater story.

Why does the word keep taking flesh?
A nameless dream
wild stratagem
wanting to shape our venture. O Gilgamesh

forever traveller, your myth brooding
in us, we grapple
with redemption's fable.
O Scheherazade healing a cuckolded king.

BELONGING

A child wanders
beyond his father's livingroom,
timorous adventurer.
Suddenly, bearings lost, he has begun to roam,
a lonely hallway of doors.

A young man flaunts
his loss of innocence, laughing off
the boy that once
didn't know a warm room was an alcove
walled in by his father's wants.

His years unwind.
A sceptic, he scanned the doors and said
on the one hand
but then on the other. Lists of choices unmade.
What was it he didn't understand?

Was his wisdom
unlived in, secondhand experience
of Peeping Tom
agog on every threshold, whipping his glance
between the frame and jamb?

Guarding his freedom
he shrugs if others pass through the door
of a chosen sanctum,
as though he doesn't know he's chosen a corridor,
this long and draughty room.

But still a question:
how, knowing every argument and angle,
to find a way in,
to tread wittingly over one door's saddle
into a room of belonging?

UNDERWORLD

Mid-morning. Beyond my blinded window
a day of creation is playing its show,
its theatre of noise. After elevenses
roofers hoist metal ladders against
a nearby gable, down a lane
children are chanting *cowardy cowardy
custard*; my neighbour must by now
be pegging her rainbow of towels on a line.

All day to do it and nothing done.
Three other books opened, begun
and abandoned; days of no purpose,
blank canvases, nadir of choices
unmade or deferred, nagging self-pity,
endless wavering and analysis. A scan
of newspaper columns fancies 'An Arabian
company requires a dynamic... (only

under twentyfives need apply)'.
Clockwatched hours weigh a century.
All day to do it and nothing done.
Is there nothing new under the sun?
Here is spiral of dark irony:
a dread of transience begins a despair
which in turn makes time unbearable.
Chaucer named *a synne of accidie*

this see-saw anguish: a thwarted will,
a clotted mind struggling to a standstill.
And meaning seizes up. *Dip your bread
in mustard* the laneway children said.
Are our days just moments that appear
and disappear or is every act heir
to an act and time that gathering river
where histories run? Wake up, sleeper!

I turn over, glazing my mind
with fragments. My tongue begins to thicken.
All the flow has gone to earth.
Ground waters stir underneath,
between soil and rock through sandstones
and shales a spring gargles against
a flag's stern underside. I dream
I'm shifting slabs from over a source.

PROBING

And there is no knowing
the weight that weighed, the agony that drove
a mind beyond its edges. Although disavowing
daylight, was he still begging love
by that dark going?

A child, a vague
signal of trouble — a threat inbred —
his name had seemed charged with guilt by lineage
'the eyes and temperament' they said
'his spitting image!'

A little older
I recall a visitor warm with charm:
'Remember I am both uncle and godfather'
he laughed, stretching a gentle arm
around my shoulder.

For years the same
lavishness: a windfall cheque 'just a token
of affection!'. I'd almost forgotten the capricious gleam
in his eye when suddenly a broken
man came

flamboyant in despair.
I knew his moods, his jerky semaphores
of warning, struggled to answer 'What does it matter?',
strove vainly to hold doors
of trust ajar.

At first the narrow
seed of terror, a tribesman's fear,
such an end might coax their kin into a burrow
of dark; I'm afraid his ghost might steer
too near the marrow.

That blotting out
I search again, summon his generosity —
uncle and godfather remember! And did I doubt
the gentle arm stirring pity
like water in a drought?

An arm now cleaning
shafts, unclogging disused conduits,
compassion at such an exit probes an opening
in old wells; shared genes and spirits
cry out for meaning.

Our lives reverberate.
As though by proxy beyond the frontiers
I have visited the blackness of his forever night
and now return to double-live arrears
of fragile sunlight.

VISION

Hollowness of eyes with no
more tears; brittle vessel
that won't weep from its clay.

Imprints, traces, shadows
of all who suffered summon
my crying. Need into need.

Breakdown of self,
cleansing of sight,
watering to the roots:
oneness with everything.

HIGH TIDE

O goddess life gather me into your flow!
White horses ride high into the taking shore —
who's winner, who's loser in such a love-making?
The mind resists a moment, hanging like a bird
caught in crosswinds. So this is high tide.
I wonder as I walk Bull Island's ribbon of sand
is this the morning Gilgamesh wept because a world
held back its secret *but be merry and make your bride
happy in your embrace, this too is the lot of man.*
A chaos of foam recedes, look an archipelago,
islands of froth dividing, a genesis in water,
creation's second day, a world reshaping!

Dunlins wheel in unison, fledgling consortium
snatching in their span plays of light's mystery,
they tilt out of dark undersides of splendour.
And still the earth melodeoned by the moon's
gravities moves a tide. Near the waterside
an old man sits to watch the sun's climb
to another summer; tumbling, tumbling in the dunes
tip and tig children still laugh and hide
in their laughter. *Is everything marvellous in its time?
So who then can number the clouds in wisdom?*
Goddess life sighs dizzily in her ecstasy —
'love me!'. I heave sweetly into our surrender.

FREEDOM

Enough was enough. We flew
nets of old certainties,
all that crabbed grammar
of the predictable. Unentangled,
we'd soar to a language
     of our own.

Freedom. We sang of freedom
(travel lightly, anything goes)
and somehow became strangers
to each other, like gabblers
at cross purposes, builders
     of Babel.

Slowly I relearn a *lingua*,
shared overlays of rule,
lattice of memory and meaning,
our latent images, a tongue
at large in an endlessness
     of sentences unsaid.

THOSE WE FOLLOW

The best said little, yet enough to signal praise
the best said least, never laid too heavy a hand;
just a glance of light, a path I might find,
but I followed false signs, stumbled into byways.

At last I retrace, begin the haul again —
the double task that probes the double faith of loss
before gain. And then a patient glow of progress.
I so wanted them to know, to call to them:

O, look what I have done! But they have gone
beyond the bend and out of sight. I sway
an instant, peering ahead; a voice resonates:
steady as you go, you carry someone's beacon.

TOUCHSTONE

Surely I'm not alone in this? Everyone
remembers some first fragrance — or was it
a colour or sound strumming the cranium?

My parents sat up night after night
to vigil my fever. Delirium and eternity
smudged into weeks I'd lie and wait,

gathering nerve for an August afternoon,
when at last I'm promised a whole hour
by my window, where the days still shone.

The curtains breathe an aroma of Autumn.
The latticed speaker of a big orange-dialled
wireless croons and fills the bedroom.

Red gladioli rage busily in the garden,
blooming their loud swords, pickets
on paradise. It must have happened then.

And nothing else would ever do again:
blaze of an instant, infallible gauge
before we'd given it a meaning or name.

Or do some forget? Do some skate
easily along the rims of gloom?
Dark is darker after the light.

I crave take-off, long flights inward,
a glowing, height after height, hum
of a moment flown Icarusly near the sun.

RETURN

O river, indomitable woman
unearthing a course, a stubborn
momentum looping, your shovel
gouging by stealth; determined,
you scoop your bed — a lover
leaving no stone unturned.

I knew a half-bend of this river,
a slow arching of the Dodder
alongside a park-path between
two busy bridges, an elbow
of adventure where my Captain
Imagination sailed the Shenandoah.

Schoolchildren had we begun
to gauge the swerve of wonder?
Who said truth was a fact?
The longest reach is the Nile:
somehow my Dodder contracted,
like a love not quite to scale.

Perhaps to know is to regain
the loss of gain; as when
he knew each loop and eyot
Twain mourned for mystery:
turning master and pilot,
had he lost his Mississippi?

In the same September sun
I skim a sliver of stone,
to count in water ricochets
decades now worn older:
I unwind into come-what-may,
an Atlas untensing his shoulders.

Is this then the return?
But the river hurries on.
No regrets. Wherever a curve
wanders at large, her waters
close up a hoop, cutting off
ingrown meanders of remorse.

O mover, driver of water,
channel of unplanned demeanour,
beautiful rover, you wriggle
of river, my Dodder of youth,
endless hunger for the possible
living from source to mouth.

V

REROOTING

This is travelling out to where

a curved adventure
splashes on planes of sunlight to become
one perfectly remembered room...

Anne Stevenson

Journeys
Beginnings
A Presence
An Unfolding
Squall
The Other Voice
Out of the Blue
St. Brigid's Cross
While You Are Talking
Hindsight
A Circle

JOURNEYS

Does something mischievous scheme to leave
an infinity in each face of a single muse?
Does a man know every woman since Eve
travelling the ring of one lover's moods?
Maybe we choose a point to enter
the circle; then slant our painstaking
angle, a slope to the flaring centre,
a focussed abandon, a slow love-making.
Strange, at the rim it seemed we left
a whirl of choices beyond recall;
in the hub's flush all angles met,
a needlepoint where winner takes all:
a wheel is the rim of many ways,
spokes of intensity, journeys to the blaze.

BEGINNINGS

A wing stirs in its sheath. Now it seems
all the fumblings of the larva years prophesied
this moment; under a crust our dreams
uncurl, eager again to dart and glide.
Still the giddy phase before the flight
when the gravity of self holds a little back;
once bitten, twice shy, we just might
dally in our shell, a last minute back-track.
All or nothing. We shed our last alibi
as when the insect nymph dares to prize
open unwanted skins, love's dragonfly
stretches its veinlike wings into the sunrise.
Two wings interlocked, the flight begun,
a speck of news flickers under the sun.

A PRESENCE

Idle with pleasure, I let my misty gaze
find its slow way through the subdued
light to where the contour of a porcelain vase,
busy in silent meditation, alludes to you.
Along the dressing table a ceramic bazaar
of creams, moistures, lotions, ointments,
an exotic row of shapely pots and jars
stoppers the scents and vapours of a presence.
Your spirit travels in such lovely earthenware,
at ease in its clay, a vessel well turned,
cajoling the mind down from a castle in the air
back to the sweeter givenness of your world.
Still, like a wooer on his first sightseeing,
I relish the emblems, your haberdashery of being.

AN UNFOLDING

An eager new shoot, I brimmed with sunkissed
boyish dreams of where my years might glide,
little knowing how a bitter frost could decide
the date of flowering, our story's turn and twist.
Damage done, the self — that secret strategist —
staunched its wound, anguished out of bruised pride
visions of Utopias, worlds cut and dried.
The heart, a frosted bud, tightened like a fist.
Your love — though it disclaims what it achieves —
unclenches me, keeping a watch, loyal yet unblinking,
full of yeses, fresh starts or that silent act
of merely being easy and ample as a mid-spring
coaxing open the horse-chestnut's sweetsmelling bract
to lodge sunlight deep in the fabric of its leaves.

SQUALL

A misunderstanding we should but didn't broach
rankles, then flares; one loaded remark
rocks our world. Strangers, we stand stark
and alone as words sweep us in whirlwinds of reproach.
Old sores glare. Once more the soul's search:
why did we risk the naked light or embark
on this journey? Yet why forestall dark with dark?
Buffeted we ride the storm's pitch and lurch.
A squall clears, the sky lifts — our kisses
timid tokens of amnesty as the purged air
breathes its sweet aftermath. Diffident, we pledge
never again like fledgling lovers still aware
how the great fluke of love poises on a knife-edge;
even the turning earth trembles on its axis.

THE OTHER VOICE

You came lean and taut, a barrage of innocence.
I remember a bluster of haughtiness hiding a boy
still dazed with childhood hurts, a man tense
with desire; slowly I thawed and rocked you in joy.
You mocked our speck of being; I showed instead
of dust a galaxy whirling in the sunbeam's eye;
you cried at the size of eternity, I hushed and said
eons count as kisses under a lover's sky.
No half-measures then. I have made this island
of life a kingdom. Have I stinted your ease
or pleasure? No, how could a woman understand
that men still talk of freedom to go as they please?
My love is your freedom. Do or die or downfall,
it's all or nothing and I have chosen all.

OUT OF THE BLUE

Nothing can explain this adventure — let's say a quirk
of fortune steered us together — we made our covenants,
began this odyssey of ours, by hunch and guesswork,
a blind date where foolish love consented in advance.
No my beloved, neither knew what lay behind the frontiers.
You told me once you hesitated: *a needle can waver,*
then fix on its pole; I am still after many years
baffled that the needle's gift dipped in my favour.
Should I dare to be so lucky? Is this a dream?
Suddenly in the commonplace that first amazement seizes
me all over again — a freak twist to the theme,
subtle jazz of the new familiar, trip of surprises.
Gratuitous, beyond our fathom, both binding and freeing,
this love re-invades us, shifts the boundaries of our being.

ST. BRIGID'S CROSS

All business, a sheaf of rushes cradled carefully
in your arms, a culotte swaying daylight in your stride
you hurry indoors to set about a February ceremony
shaping your namesake's token, flourish for Spring's bride.
A city child I'd seen the crosses above doors but missed
this rite, so it always seemed that something in the stretch
of those curious jerky arms with bows on their wrists,
honey-coloured and brittle, beckoned to a world beyond reach.
Lank green stalks crisscross their sign language;
seasons of hands are working that saint's emblem,
a lineage moving in your fingers; instinctively you bridge
worlds kneeling on a Dublin floor to knot a rush stem.
I watch you weave as the rush twists and reappears,
a freshcut badge of love, this nexus of our years.

WHILE YOU ARE TALKING

While you are talking though I seem all ears
forgive me if you notice a stray see-through
look; on tiptoe behind the eyes' frontiers
I am spying, wondering at this mobile you.
Sometimes nurturer, praise-giver to the male,
caresser of failures, mother earth, breakwater
to my vessel, suddenly you'll appear frail —
in my arms I'll cradle you like a daughter.
Now soul-pilot and I confess redemptress,
turner of new leaves, reshaper of a history;
then the spirit turns flesh — playful temptress
I untie again ribbons of your mystery.
You shift and travel as only a lover can;
one woman and all things to this one man.

HINDSIGHT

Though thankful, at first finding the glare too bright
I flinched — as when the longsought sun comes,
shrivelled by too much winter, the core numbs;
timorous in the glow — a sudden bout of stagefright.
But it's all summer now. Your lavish sunlight
wakes and stretches these Van Winkle limbs;
I nuzzle up to the warmth, the love-sap brims
over, plush with the freedom of second sight.
Yet sometimes across the moon sky a sullen
cloud laments those angry years — hauteur
of hurt — when spring slid without my noticing
the willow covers its blossoms with silver fur
as hedge-sparrows flirted and jerked their wings
and the east wind scattered the alder catkin's pollen.

A CIRCLE

After lights out, weary from the long regime,
remember the dressing gowns, the illicit tiptoe
to whisper at the radiator hugging its last glow
until nabbed by the flashlight's accusing beam.
The first Christmas break passed in a daydream,
the rooms dwarfed, home become a sideshow
to a cosmos of corridors and braggadocio, as though
the garment of childhood had slit along its seam.
Now I love to watch the lighthouse at Howth
flash its codes to steer ships past our gable,
to gossip in the dark with you my bed and boarder
and marvel at how, like tortoises in an Aesop fable
our years have coiled their slow circles of growth;
a world brought back to scale, a house to order.

VI

OPENING OUT

The sun! The sun! And all we can become!
And the time for running to the moon!
In the long fields, I leave my father's eye;
And shake the secrets from my deepest bones...

Theodore Roethke

Disclosure
Grantchester Meadows
Motet
Train Journey
Kinsmen
Matins
Perspectives
Memory
Hail! Madam Jazz
Child

DISCLOSURE

Remember how at school we folded and unfolded
sheets from a jotter, scissored chunky *m*s and *n*s,
a saw-edge,
a clump of paper squared, melodeoned.
Then delight as it reopens
a fulness of design, transfigured wounds
unfolding in a page
berries, acorns.

The moment's contours scatter in the light.
A crossbeam gathers in pattern and fringe,
traces of passion,
hologram of thought, memory's freight
until a beam re-throws the image,
an intensity unpacking stripe and whorl;
each fraction
an implicit all.

Acorns of memories, berries of dreams.
Does every pilgrim's tale sleep in one moment?
Some inbred
whole uncodes in a tree's limbs,
spreads in slow workings of environment.
Soil, air, water, sun quicken
a word in the seed.
Time thickens.

GRANTCHESTER MEADOWS

Across Grantchester Meadows, May has snowed
cow parsnip, hawthorn, chestnut; a stone's throw
from here the Cam grooves slowly towards King's.
An English heaven: 'My real life began since
I came to Grantchester. I eat strawberries and honey.
A perfectly glorious time. Think only this of me.'

I see you Rupert Brooke blazered, flannelled,
a strolling presence in this albescent funnel
of young Summer or picnicking under an oak
with Darwin's granddaughters: 'We used to talk
wearily about art, suicide, the sex problem'.
Übermensch, libido, absinthe, fin de siècle.

A 100 rings in an oak which may have seen
George Herbert brooding by the *Came* or Milton
explaining the ways of God now Galileo's sun
no longer danced attendance on our world. Newton,
did you some midsummer hatch along this path
laws to bring our universe back to earth?

'Certainly I approve of war at any price,
it kills the unnecessary.' Evenings of tennis
and cricket. It's the Aegean 1913:
'My poem is to be about the existence of England'.
Dead before the Dardanelles. A circle closes;
the hawthorn almost in bloom, the oak leafless.

Wars. Disillusion. Certainty a fallen idol,
our daylight turns a dice-dance of potential.
Turmoil of change as an old order dies
into us. Herbert must have known the crux.
Does the slow-leafing oak trust without proof?
I know the ways of learning yet I love.

Ghost Brooke you could be my father's father,
yet I'm your elder. Ride my Aeneas shoulder
as Grantchester blooms a lover's carte-blanche,
another innocence. Do you remember how strange
the fulness of the riddle seemed? *The acorn can't
explain the oak, the oak explains the acorn.*

MOTET

O my white-burdened Europe, across
so many maps greed zigzags. One voice
and the nightmare of a dominant chord:
defences, self-mirroring, echoings, myriad
overtones of shame. Never again one voice.
Out of malaise, out of need our vision cries.

Turmoil of change, our slow renaissance.
All things share one breath. We listen:
clash and resolve, webs and layers of voices.
And which voice dominates or is it chaos?
My doubting earthling, tiny among the planets
does a lover of one voice hear more or less?

Infinities of space and time. Melody fragments;
a music of compassion, noise of enchantment.
Among the inner parts something open,
something wild, a long rumour of wisdom
keeps winding into each tune: *cantus firmus*,
fierce vigil of contingency, love's congruence.

TRAIN JOURNEY

As a boy I was sure that the track's anapaest
kept narrating each passenger's tale: like a charge
of experience, each face was a secret released.

Soon we rushed over a bridge's trestled brick-arch,
almost loving the dare and danger of a fall
till the train suddenly hurtled into shafts of dark.

Who would make it through this funnel
of night? Was it too long to believe
light might be waiting in the eye of the tunnel?

Some would go under in the dark. I grieve
for a fellow-traveller, a woman taut
as a violin, lavishing her girth of life

into song. Too near the edge and overwrought:
But how should I sing unless I burn?
Long afterwards I'd discover she'd fought

to the death her loneliness, flitting in turn
from friend's door to door. If I'd known
could I have comforted her? Was our sojourn

together a barrier to an inaccessible zone
of once intimacies? Always I remember
a voice spilling *from clear daylight till dawn.*

Like a child half awake on a morning in midsummer
I'm rubbing the dark from my eyes. Unbelievable
how the light is despatching its trees like ambassadors

that glide by our windows with an urgent epistle.
And I think I then knew that a train's undersong
began mourning the traveller whose story I'd tell.

KINSMEN

Father used love to walk the block on Sunday;
skipping along a garden wall I found a slot
where our street met the road. 'The builder forgot
a brick' — my father shrugged but I insisted why?

Why? Why did that builder leave such a hole
just where our street met with the main road?
Why didn't Father know why? Through childhood
I am sure I puzzled over that slit in a wall.

Then I must have forgotten. Nearing the age
he begot me, I think I heard someone explain
how the Hopi gathered their older children
in a hut to watch the gods' arrival in a village.

Painted ogres would circle, dance and howl,
then entering the hut they unmasked to expose
fathers and kinsmen playing at being gods.
I began remembering a peephole in childhood's wall

before the anger of disenchantment, before the flood
of our arrogance had swept both wall and garden.
So often since I have wanted to beg his pardon,
or at least to say how now I maybe understood.

Lately strolling the block again together
I asked nudgingly if he remembered that hole?
But he stares: 'Son, I am growing so forgetful!';
I fumble to link his arm, my ageing brother.

MATINS

Segovia, guitarman, I know your prayer:
never mind, Lord, treasures laid up,
leave me this street where a greengrocer
draws a striped awning over his show
of yellow buttocked melons and blowzy peaches.

I can idle here by the corner, watch
children busy chalking a hopscotch
on the pavement or eavesdrop on schoolboys
bragging and smoking by the railway
bridge where young executives scurry.

A very ordinary mortal I gaze
boyishly at women's turquoise rings
as their hands touch in talk, delight
in loose cottons, linen blazers,
perfumes hugging air as they pass.

O polyphony of being, doing, bliss.
My senses feast. I breathe and am.
O hankerer after the irrevocable.
O plucker at words, colours, chords.
Are they real? Do we dream it all?

Gilgamesh, Odysseus, Mad Quixote,
wanderers relive in us your daylight.
And hey! what stranger down the line
moves to this rhythm, whose moment
twangs in the blood? Good morning, Segovia.

PERSPECTIVES

1

Like pegs, our forearms held the skein's coil.
Arcs of the knitter's hand unloop
and ball by turn. Sweep and detail.
A feeling of beginning in childhood's wind-up
I keep on recalling. Somehow I'm between
a yarn uncoiling to a tight ball of destiny,
a ball unravelling back the promise of a skein.
Plain stitch and design; point and infinity.
Who changes the world? Oh, this and that,
strands as they happen to fall, tiny ligatures,
particular here and nows, vast loopings
of pattern, the ties and let-gos of a knot,
small X-shapes of history; our spoor and signature
a gauze of junctures, a nettedness of things.

2

Whose music? A quiver enters like a spirit,
a murmur of tension from and back
into space. A tune of trembles in catgut.
The pride of an instrument as at its beck
and call the heart vibrates: pulse-sway,
dominion of rhythm, power before the slack
and silence. 'Pride before a fall' we say,
sic transit.... Should we've been puritans,
taut, untouchable, our unshakable self-mastery
a vacuum of muteness? O noise of existence
shake in me a tone you need; sweet
friction of rosin, play me limp or tense.
Possessor of everything, owner of nothing.
Whose bow shivers its music in my string?

3
Nineteen forty-three, Tegel prison, Berlin.
I picture a face superimposed on a grill:
first widening of a smile, the mooning hairline,
something plump and composed, relentless will.
Time-servers slide; many in their armchairs
rage. Call them opters-out or captives.
Success makes history, I hear him say, *There's
no out. How will another generation live?*
The question echoes on: yardstick of ambition,
our spirit level. Hanged Flossenbürg camp,
April of forty-five. Dietrich Bonhöffer,
like an eavesdropper, I glean smuggled wisdom.
Sometimes, it was piano wire — slower than hemp.
Suffer them in the light of what they suffer.

4
Specky-four-eyes, carrots, fatso, dunce!
Jeer and name-call and how we changed it to sport,
swagger of couldn't-care-less: *sticks and stones
may break my bones, names 'll never hurt.*
But still he's there, that curly-headed boy
scrambling a pillar: *I'm the king of the castle;*
a shout of territory, the old pedestal cry
defining by rivalry. *Get down you dirty rascal.*
Always black and white. Why south, why north,
paleface or nigger or prod? I, Paddy,
dream the schoolroom globe, a balloon viewed
with a spaceman's floating glance; my heady
vision a sea with tatters and patches of earth,
our odds and ends hung on a line of latitude.

MEMORY

Again a silent room.
Doubt bows the cello
of morning. A diminished chord.
Lord Shallot to his loom
spelled to watch the river
in a mirror?
Why? While people war?
While people famish?

All the suspicions, excuses.
Where's the extravagant stillness
of a lover's mind?
Alert as madness, fierce
sojourner in a small womb's
patience. Then slowness:
rhythmic openings and closings
of woof and heddle.

Warped threads of memory
dream a weft, a journey
of doing — triple interplay.
Am I warden of filigrees,
patterns, the colours and plot,
keeper of the cloth,
the bobbin's eye, a forethought
in the shuttle's long cast?

Not even to try. A texture
of knots and intersections,
a youth ravelling its fulness,
layered music of complexity.
Cypresses sway in their spring;
the lattice and web of things
a frail morning
eastering another garden.

And the river moves:
a light, a shape, a weave.
Someone was busy in a kitchen,
someone was patching a roof,
someone was sowing wheat
or hustling the market.
Who was it noticed and forgot?
For us I've remembered.

HAIL! MADAM JAZZ

Worship, hold her a moment in thought.
Femme fatale, she shapes another face,
unveils an idol. O Never-To-Be-Caught,

O Minx beyond this mind's embrace,
Hider-Go-Seeker, Miss Unfathomable,
Demurring Lady playing at the chase.

As stars or atoms we turn, fall
towards each other's gravity. I spin
in your love's nexus, Mistress All.

Once a child of Newton's fallen
apple, I'd the measure of your ways.
My stars, my atoms, are we one?

Mischievous Strategy, Madam Jazz!
Old tunes die in metamorphosis.
Rise, fall, reawakening. I praise.

CHILD

It's evening as I pass the first garden
a day's playthings scattered in the dew:
an upturned tractor yellow and forgotten
under lupins and London pride, a blue
rubber ball wobbled to a standstill.
Did someone call 'Come on, come on
it's bedtime!' And did you stall
the lone moment of sleep, of abandon?

I know your player's garden in
and out. Behind a fence and walls
silent first growths are gathering
sap in the long uncurling falls
of a dusk. Innocent know-how
is not to know. Beyond this greenroom
there are ordeals of suspicion. I know
the rip, the pain before bloom.

This take-for-granted is your garden.
Sureness of path, stakes and wires
that hold the sweet pea, our heaven
of invention, dream-castle of desire.
Doubts are jags of bottle glass
on an orchard walltop. Bit by bit
you awaken, must learn to mistrust
these gates your father shuts at night.

An apple-bite and that garden vanishes
forever. You too will roam with Adam.
Sap in the trees' limbs still lavishes
memories. You grow to another millennium.
Is what we love what we find?
Is there somewhere a second garden,
an arbour where the quickened mind
soars between its knowing and abandon?

Will the stars you once thought your own
slide infinitely away; mischievous,
faster-than-light teams of subatoms
conspire beyond your common sense;
a universe of unfoldings and enfoldings
draw in its mystery? Part and parcel
as housekeeper not householder
will you dream, fumble with the possible?

A dangerous growth. Make or break
a lupin slits its tightlipped calyx,
London pride is living off its luck,
a rubber ball circles dark in itself.
Double-edge of nurture, of damage.
There's no undoing all our knowledge.
Bon Voyage! Where will you choose
another garden, another innocence?

BIOGRAPHICAL NOTE

Micheal O'Siadhail has been a lecturer at Trinity College Dublin and a professor at The Dublin Institute for Advanced Studies, and is now a full-time writer.

Among his previous collections are **Springnight** (1983) and **The Image Wheel** (1985)

He was awarded the Irish American Cultural Institute's prize for poetry.

A former editor of **Poetry Ireland Review** he is a member of Aosdána and of The Arts Council of the Republic of Ireland.

Springnight:

"The poems in *Springnight* are always thoughtful and often moving. Brilliant flashes of observation occur throughout this volume." — Michael O'Neill *Times Literary Supplement*

"The freshest talent from Ireland" — Frank Delaney *The Listener*

The Image Wheel:

"There is a confident assurance evident in these pages, a joyous commitment to the threads of time which poetry can weave, that suggests a major talent in the making" — Conor Kelly *Magill*